# who is worthy?